32.79

MW00953213

WILLIAM SHAKESPEARE

Essential Lives

WILLIAM
SHAKESPEARE

PLAYWRIGHT & POET

by Emma Carlson Berne

Content Consultant:
Marcela Kostihová, Assistant Professor of English
Hamline University

ABDO
Publishing Company

CREDITS

Published by ABDO Publishing Company, 8000 West 78th Street, Edina, Minnesota 55439. Copyright © 2008 by Abdo Consulting Group, Inc. International copyrights reserved in all countries. No part of this book may be reproduced in any form without written permission from the publisher. The Essential Library™ is a trademark and logo of ABDO Publishing Company.

Printed in the United States.

Editor: Jill Sherman
Copy Editor: Paula Lewis
Interior Design and Production: Rebecca Daum
Cover Design: Rebecca Daum

Library of Congress Cataloging-in-Publication Data
Berne, Emma Carlson.
 William Shakespeare / Emma Berne.
    p. cm. — (Essential lives)
 Includes bibliographical references.
 ISBN 978-1-60453-042-1
 1. Shakespeare, William, 1564-1616—Juvenile literature. 2. Dramatists, English—Early modern, 1500-1700—Biography—Juvenile literature. 3. Theater—England—History—16th century—Juvenile literature. I. Title.
 PR2895.B48 2008
 822.3'3—dc22

                                        2007030839

TABLE OF CONTENTS

William Shakespeare

WHO WAS
WILLIAM SHAKESPEARE?

William Shakespeare was an Elizabethan playwright who wrote some of the most widely praised dramas in the English language. His surviving works include 38 plays and 154 sonnets, as well as a number of other poems. His masterpieces include such works as *Hamlet*, *Macbeth*, *Romeo and Juliet*, *The Merchant of Venice*, and *Twelfth Night*. His plays continue to be performed long after his death. They are studied in classrooms everywhere and are made into films.

Despite Shakespeare's fame, little is known about him. What is known for certain about Shakespeare could be written in a few paragraphs. Yet great, thick biographies have been written about the poet for centuries.

Shakespeare Scholars

Some historical figures document every event of their lives and leave scholars with diaries, letters, essays, and musings on their innermost thoughts. Shakespeare historians have none of these. The greatest Western dramatist in history left no letters and no diaries—he did not even sign some of his plays. One of the only personal documents he left behind was his will. This lack of documentation has made Shakespeare's activities difficult to trace. However, it is not surprising that there is so little historical record left of Shakespeare. He lived 400 years ago, during a time when record keeping was scarce or careless.

Scholars look to Shakespeare's legal and church documents to learn about his life. These documents show things such as births, deaths, marriages, and land purchases. Scholars also read his plays and poems for clues about what Shakespeare might have been thinking and feeling at different stages of his life. In addition, scholars look at the letters and writings of Shakespeare's friends and associates for mentions of him.

His Own Words

Shakespeare invented dozens of his words, many of which are in common use today. Words attributed to Shakespeare include: champion, skim milk, addiction, fashionable, equivocal, gossip, green-eyed, remorseless, savagery, blanket, eyeball, and zany.

With this information, scholars then study the customs of the time. They research the lives of other people of Shakespeare's social class and occupation. They look for information regarding his friends and close companions. All these things are indicators of what Shakespeare would have been doing and who he would have been doing those things with. Despite the lack of formal documentation, many Shakespeare scholars are fairly certain of Shakespeare's activities during his life.

The Authorship Debate

Some scholars have questioned whether Shakespeare actually wrote the works that are attributed to him. Shakespeare left few personal documents, letters, or notes. This lack of documentation has led some scholars to argue that there is little or no proof that Shakespeare wrote the works attributed to him.

This view is controversial; most scholars believe there is no reason to doubt that Shakespeare is the author of his famous plays.

Other scholars have suggested a variety of people

The Plays of William Shakespeare

Comedy	History
All's Well That Ends Well	Henry IV, Part 1
As You Like It	Henry IV, Part 2
The Comedy of Errors	Henry V
Cymbeline	Henry VI, Part 1
Love's Labour's Lost	Henry VI, Part 2
Measure for Measure	Henry VI, Part 3
The Merchant of Venice	Henry VII
The Merry Wives of Windsor	King John
A Midsummer Night's Dream	Richard II
Much Ado About Nothing	Richard III
Pericles	
The Taming of the Shrew	**Tragedy**
The Tempest	Antony and Cleopatra
Troilus and Cressida	Coriolanus
Twelfth Night	Hamlet
The Two Gentlemen of Verona	Julius Caesar
The Winter's Tale	King Lear
	Macbeth
	Othello
	Romeo and Juliet
	Timon of Athens
	Titus Andronicus

who might actually be the author of Shakespeare's work: the playwright and poet Christopher Marlowe, the philosopher Francis Bacon, and a playwright, poet, and earl named Edward de Vere. Some have hypothesized that a countess named Mary Sidney or even Queen Elizabeth was the real "Shakespeare."

These are only theories, however. The author of Shakespeare's work is still assumed to be Shakespeare.

THE MYSTERY

Scholars continue to study the life of William Shakespeare. They try to uncover the mysteries of his life to learn more about the man who produced so many great works of literature. There are several periods in Shakespeare's life of which almost nothing is known at all. The mystery surrounding Shakespeare's life only adds to its intrigue.

What was Shakespeare doing during those blank periods? What inspired him? What were his feelings for his wife and children? And perhaps most importantly: Who was William Shakespeare?

Shakespeare at work in his study

William Shakespeare's birthplace

First Act

One day toward the end of April in 1564, in the English village of Stratford-upon-Avon, the cry of a newborn baby rang from the window of a large house on Henley Street. Mary Shakespeare had given birth to another child.

A New Baby

Mary and her husband, John, must have been pleased. The new baby boy was strong and healthy. In those days, infants often died in the first hours or weeks of life. John and Mary's first child had only lived a little over a year, and their second daughter, Margaret, died when she was only a few months old. They hoped their son would survive.

On April 26, the Shakespeare family dressed in their best clothes and walked together to the parish church. The vicar, John Bretchgirdle, christened the new baby: William Shakespeare.

Little William was a lucky boy. His father was an important man in town and the family lived in one of the finest houses in Stratford. It had six rooms and a workshop for John's glove-making business. The upper and lower stories were connected by a ladder. The kitchen contained a huge stone fireplace, which heated the entire house in the winter. In the downstairs parlor, John and Mary's large bed was displayed. In Shakespeare's time, people spent a

Stratford Neighbors

There were many merchants in Stratford, but the area in which the Shakespeares lived was mostly populated by those who dealt in cloth and leather. Another glover, Gilbert Bradley, lived across the little stream that ran by the Shakespeares' Henley Street house. William Wedgwood, a tailor, and Richard Hornby, a blacksmith, also lived nearby. A clothes seller in Stratford, William Smith, was William Shakespeare's godfather.

great deal of money, if they could, on the family bed and considered it a prized possession.

JOHN SHAKESPEARE

In addition to making gloves from calves' leather and lambskin, John Shakespeare was the bailiff in Stratford. This was considered an important job. The bailiff was the town official in charge of inspecting and approving visitors to the village. He also gave permission for different activities, heard complaints from the villagers, and set the price for corn—the staple food for the people.

John was respected and well liked. He did, however, have a secret. For a long time, John had kept an illegal side business. He bought and sold wool even though he was not an authorized wool dealer. This was called wool brogging. As a glover, John was only permitted to buy and sell leather.

In spite of his secret, William's father had worked hard to create the comfortable life he and his family led in Stratford. John was born in the

The Henley Street House Today

Until 1806, the Henley Street house where William grew up was owned by descendents of the Shakespeare family. In 1847, the Shakespeare Birthplace Trust bought the house. It has remained a tourist attraction ever since.

village of Snitterfield, just more than four miles (6 km) from Stratford. He was the son of a tenant farmer, Richard Shakespeare. Richard rented the land he farmed from the landowner, Robert Arden. Although John's family was not terribly poor when he was growing up, John did not want to be a farmer. He wanted to become a tradesman.

In the 1550s, John moved to Stratford, where he apprenticed himself to a glove maker. He learned to work with a soft, light-colored leather from the skins of deer, horses, goats, sheep, and dogs. He became expert enough to take over the business. John established himself as a solid, responsible man in town. He soon took his first role as a public official: ale taster. Each week, John visited all of the ale makers and bakers in town. He inspected and tasted the quality of the beer and the bread. He even had a little house on Henley Street that he had bought shortly after arriving in town. Now the only thing he needed was a wife.

MARY SHAKESPEARE

John returned to Snitterfield. He visited Mary Arden, the daughter of his father's landlord. Mary was a member of an old, respected family. Some of the Ardens were wealthy noblemen. Mary's father, Robert, was well-off but not particularly wealthy. He was a farmer who kept chickens, pigs, and beehives. He also farmed wheat and barley. When he died in 1556, he left Mary almost all of his land and fortune.

That same year, John Shakespeare bought the house neighboring his own on Henley Street. He then hired workmen to connect the two into a fine double residence with space for a glove shop. Most likely, John and Mary were wed at the nearby church in Aston Cantlow around 1557.

Leather Making

Making gloves as John Shakespeare did required excellent leather. John not only made the gloves, he produced the leather.

When the skins arrived, they were dirty. John would soak them for two or three days in water. Then he rinsed them and painted them with lime to remove the hair and flesh. "Liming" lasted several weeks. Afterward, the hair and flesh could be scraped off with a dull knife. The skins were then soaked in a mixture of dog droppings and urine. These chemicals broke down the tough fibers and made the skins soft. The skins were rinsed again and placed in a tub of bran and water to remove the lime before being scraped again.

When the skins were ready for tanning, they were soaked first in a salt and chemical solution and then in a flour and egg yolk mixture. This kept the leather from shrinking as it dried. The skins were twisted to soften them and laid flat to dry in the sun. The leather was then covered with damp sawdust and rubbed across a blade to further soften it.

Paring was the final step. John carefully shaved off any uneven parts. Finally, the leather was ready to dye, waterproof, and cut into shape.

Even though the family was financially comfortable, Mary Shakespeare would have spent her days in the usual activities of a woman with a house and garden. With the help of a servant, she was responsible for the washing, sewing, and baking. Many families brewed their own beer, which everyone drank, including children. Mary would measure the hops and barley for the ale and tend it while it fermented. She spun all of the yarn for the family's clothes using a hand spindle, wove it on her loom, and sewed it into garments. She milked the cows, made the butter and the cheese, and tended the garden. In the autumn, she joined the rest of the family in harvesting the hay for the livestock.

It was hard work, and there was not often a break from the routine. But sometimes, the high call of a horn would echo through the streets of the village. Everyone would stop what they were doing; a group of players had arrived.

Plays and Players

Accompanied by a lively tune on a flute and drums, with brilliant colors flying from a ragged banner, the actors would parade through the main street, their costume and prop wagon trailing

Gloves and Shakespeare

Though he did not follow his father into the business, William Shakespeare clearly knew a lot about leather and gloves. In many of his plays, he makes references to styles and fitting of gloves, as well as descriptions of different types of leather.

In *The Merry Wives of Windsor*, a character asks, "Does he not wear a great round beard, like a glover's paring-knife?"[1] In *Romeo and Juliet*, the character Mercutio tells Romeo, "O, here's a wit of cherevel [a type of leather], that stretches from an inch narrow to an ell [forty-five inches] broad!"[2]

behind. They were on their way to the bailiff's house to request permission to perform.

Performance was very common in England. Since most people could not read, they depended on plays, storytelling, poetry recitals, and singers for their entertainment. Townspeople would gather to hear the latest story or ballad from a traveling storyteller or musician. The people of Stratford created their own performances too. Most holidays were marked by a parade with people dressed in their best clothes, marching through town playing instruments and shouting. They also would dance and put on amateur skits.

Professional actors did not always perform in playhouses. Many small troupes toured the countryside, setting up in villages for a few days to perform. They would perform in the homes of rich people or in the open air. These troupes were regarded with excitement by the townspeople and suspicion by the authorities. To protect themselves from accusations of being criminals, troupes found members of the nobility to sponsor them. An earl or a duke, or even a queen or a king, would become the troupe's patron, or protector. A patron would give the players a small yearly salary and cast-off clothes for costumes. In return, the troupe would be named for the patron and perform for him or her upon their request.

In 1569, when William was five years old, Stratford was visited by two acting troupes: the Queen's Men and the Earl of Worcester's Men. As was the custom, they went to the bailiff's house to request permission to perform.

The traveling players' first performance in a city was always called the Mayor's Play. The authorities in town, including the bailiff, were the honored guests. John Shakespeare and his family would have been invited to these performances. In the town common, they would watch as the actors danced, recited, and fought with their swords and daggers.

During this period in England, the plays most often performed in villages were "morality plays." These plays demonstrated what happened when people sinned or disobeyed the authorities.

Characters with names such as "Youth" or "Manhood" misbehaved with characters named "Ignorance" or "Riot" before they learned their lesson and made friends with "Virtue" or "Patience." These plays allowed the audience to escape from their daily lives and enjoy a simple story. The wicked characters were their favorites. Audiences cheered the loudest when Youth and Riot created mischief and havoc before Virtue stepped in.

Years later, when William was a playwright, he would remember how popular these plays were. In writing his own plays, he would borrow certain character types and plots from the morality plays. He would make sure that his plays were fun, lively, and full of humor everyone could understand.

An Example of a Morality Play

Everyman is a morality play that was written in the fifteenth century. In the play, the character Death finds the character Everyman to make him account for himself to God. Everyman asks his friends Fellowship, Kindred, Cousin, Knowledge, and Goods to accompany him. They all refuse. Only the neglected Good Deeds will help him justify himself before God.

*Before formal playhouses became common, acting troupes
would perform in the streets.*

An Elizabethan woman works in a kitchen.

GROWING UP
IN STRATFORD

ventually, Mary Shakespeare would bear
eight children, five of whom would live
to adulthood: William, Gilbert, Joan, Richard,
and Edmund. Little William probably helped his
mother with chores and played games such as bowls,

prisoner's base, hide-and-seek, and chess with his siblings.

All of the children were expected to obey their parents without question. They served their mother and father at the table. They removed their hats before speaking. If they disobeyed, they could expect to be punished with beatings.

When William was about six years old, he was old enough to start school. Stratford had a very good grammar school, the King's New School. Although none of its records have survived, most scholars believe that William was a student. His writing shows that he received an education and this school was the most likely place.

During this period, many people did not know how to read or write. Books were rare and paper was expensive. Some people, especially poor people, never even saw a book. Mary could not read or write; she always signed her name with a mark. John would have known how to read in order to be the bailiff. However,

The Shakespeare Siblings

Historians know little about William's sister and brothers. Gilbert was a tradesman in Stratford, probably in the glove business with his father, and died when he was 45 years old. Joan married a man named William Hart and had four children. She and her family lived in the Henley Street house until her death. Little is known about Richard except that he died in 1613. Edmund followed his famous brother to London and became an actor. He died in that city at the age of 27.

because he signed his name with a mark, he probably could not write. John and Mary would have wanted better for their children.

Once William started school, he rose early, about four or five o'clock in the morning. In the dark, he gathered his materials: school texts, a few sheets of expensive paper, a feather quill for writing, and a little bottle of ink. Students had to bring their own candles, because lessons would begin before sunrise and end after dark. They also brought firewood to feed the school fireplace.

All of the children had to know how to read and write English before they could enter the grammar school. Because his parents could not write, William would have attended a small petty school, or elementary school, for a year or two before starting at the King's New School. This was common for children from well-off families. Small schools were usually conducted in the local chapels. At the petty school, William learned to read the alphabet from a hornbook.

The Schoolboy

William Shakespeare makes frequent references to school in his plays. In *As You Like It*, a character named Jacques offers a description that shows how Shakespeare may have felt about his own school days: "Then the whining schoolboy, with his satchel / And shining morning face, creeping like a snail / Unwillingly to school."[1] However, by the language of Shakespeare's plays we can tell that he was a very educated man. It is hard to believe that Shakespeare would dislike school so much when he owed his career to it.

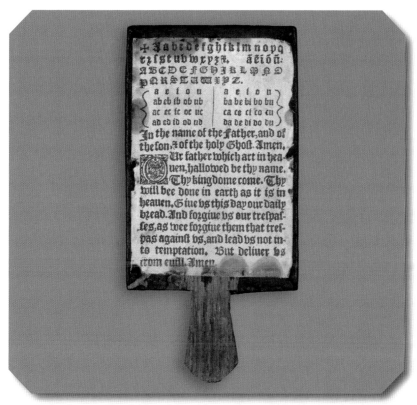

Students at King's New School learned to read from a hornbook similar to this one.

A hornbook was a sheet of paper printed with the letters glued to a wooden paddle and covered with a clear sheet of horn. William was taught to copy the letters and to read the catechism, a piece of religious writing that summarized the basic beliefs of Christianity. The catechism was the first words all children were taught.

Becoming a Schoolboy

King's New School was located above the guild hall just a quarter mile (.4 km) from Henley Street. The schoolmaster would have recorded William's name in the register and agreed to take him as a pupil for the fee of four pence—about six dollars today.

Forty-two boys ranging in age from seven to fifteen sat in rows on hard wooden benches, their books spread out before them. School began at six o'clock in the morning. The room was lit by candlelight. Prayers were followed by lessons until nine o'clock. Only then could the boys have a breakfast of bread and ale. The boys studied again until eleven o'clock, when everyone was allowed to return home for lunch. When lessons started again, everyone would study with the aid of their candles until five o'clock.

Teaching methods of the time were very different from today. The schoolmaster would drill the students repeatedly. They memorized verbs and passages and repeated them back. They sat perfectly still on their benches and had to pay attention. If they misbehaved or did not know their lessons, they were beaten with a stick. At the time, people generally agreed that beating schoolchildren was good and helped them learn. Sometimes, in training classes for teachers, a young schoolmaster would have to demonstrate how well he could beat a child.

Almost all of William's education at the King's New School focused around the study of Latin. Reading and writing in Latin were considered important skills

Plautus and Terence

William Shakespeare and other schoolboys frequently performed the plays of the Romans Titus Maccius Plautus and Publius Terentius Afer, or Terence. Plautus was born around 254 BCE and Terence around 195 or 185 BCE. Terence wrote six comic plays in his lifetime and Plautus wrote 21. Plautus was also one of the first known playwrights to have his characters sing and dance onstage during the performance.

Shakespeare recognized the appeal of these writers as he modeled some of his plays on theirs. Plautus, for instance, often had a set of identical twins as characters to add comical confusion. Shakespeare also used twin characters. In his play *Comedy of Errors*, he even had two sets of twins. Both Shakespeare and Plautus often wrote of the relationship between a silly master and a clever servant. Shakespeare also used characters straight from Plautus's plays, altering them only a little to appeal to a Christian audience.

In one of Terence's plays, a character speaks about the nature of humanity. For a playwright such as Shakespeare, who wrote about all sorts of human conditions and was loved by people of all classes, Terence seems a natural role model.

that the educated should possess. Latin is a complicated language. As a grown man, Shakespeare would sprinkle his plays and poems with Latin words and references.

Most likely, young William first began to appreciate the power of the spoken word while he attended King's New School. The art of speaking aloud, or oratory, was considered very important. Students were expected to memorize famous speeches and texts and recite them before the class.

Shakespeare and Nature

William Shakespeare's writing shows that he knew a lot about the names of flowers and plants as well as their different uses. He writes admiringly of the local celebrations that were connected to the cycle of the seasons. The villagers would hold festivities and dances to celebrate the first of May or the completion of the harvest. Many writers in Shakespeare's time thought these country customs were beneath them.

A Sense for the Stage

The school may have been the first place that William Shakespeare acted in a play. Playacting was a common activity, and students all over England performed plays in Latin to help them learn the language. The plays of the Roman poets Plautus and Terence were especially popular. The two schoolmasters who taught during the time Shakespeare attended school were specially trained in teaching through drama. They almost certainly taught their students to act.

Queen Elizabeth I

Shakespeare spent his early life in Stratford.

TROUBLES AND JOYS

illiam turned 13 years old in 1577.
While there is little documentation
of his life at this time, William would have been on
the verge of completing his education at the King's
New School. By this age, students could speak and

write Latin, had read the Roman scholars Cicero and Quintilian, and could recite entire passages of Homer and Vergil. *Metamorphoses* by the Roman poet Ovid was one of William's favorites. In the eyes of those in Stratford, William Shakespeare would have been an educated young man. But the peaceful days of learning at school, doing chores at home, and practicing archery with his friends were almost over.

Two unfortunate events happened to John Shakespeare around this time. The first was an economic recession. Money was tight. Fewer customers were buying gloves at the Shakespeare workshop. In addition, the farmers and butchers who supplied John with skins and other materials began charging higher prices because of their own financial difficulties.

CRACKDOWN ON WOOL BROGGING

Under other circumstances, John probably would have been all right during this difficult time. He was a wealthy man with property from Stratford through the surrounding Forest of Arden. Unfortunately, about the same time as the recession began, the authorities announced a crackdown on wool broggers, the illegal wool dealers. The country was in the midst of a national wool shortage, and Queen Elizabeth's Privy Council determined the broggers contributed to the problem.

John had already been warned twice to end his illegal side business. In better times, and without pressure from the Privy Council, his fellow town leaders had been willing to overlook his wool brogging. In early 1580, the Privy Council ordered all known wool broggers to post a 100-pound bond to ensure that they would stop their illegal trading.

John began missing town

Catholic or Protestant?

In 1558, Elizabeth I became Queen of England. She was a Protestant and after she was crowned, pressure was placed on the country's Catholics to convert to Protestantism. Catholicism became illegal and many Catholics were forced to go underground. Tensions between the two groups were high, and Catholics were frequently tried and executed.

Some scholars have found evidence that suggests the Shakespeare family may have been Catholic and secretly maintained their faith throughout William's lifetime. Mary Shakespeare's family, the Ardens, were known to be practicing Catholics.

In 1606, when William's daughter Susanna was an adult, she was listed as one who refused to take the Protestant communion. This refusal was a common sign of the Catholic faith.

A tract asserting Catholic faith and signed by John Shakespeare was found hidden in the rafters of the Henley Street house. However, it was not uncommon during this time for citizens such as John Shakespeare to declare that they were Catholic on paper when they actually accepted the Protestant religion. People were afraid of being punished for their religion if Protestantism was suddenly condemned. By claiming they were both Catholic and Protestant, they could avoid any danger.

council meetings for the first time in two decades. He and his family stopped attending church regularly. They were beginning to lose some of their social status. For awhile, John's good friends on the council protected him. They made excuses for him when he was absent and refrained from fining him. They even kept his name on the official rolls for almost a decade after he stopped going to meetings.

In November 1578, the Shakespeares' family finances were in serious trouble. John and Mary were forced to mortgage 56 acres (23 ha) of meadow and pastureland in the village of Wilmcote. The land had been left to Mary by her father as part of her wedding dowry. Bit by bit, John sold off some of his other houses and land; he mortgaged others.

Leaving School

When William turned 14 years old, his education at the King's New School would end. His father could pay an additional five pounds for him to continue on and learn Greek. However, considering their financial situation, it is unlikely that the Shakespeares could afford the extra fee. William was needed, no doubt, in the glove shop, helping his father and brothers with the business.

The family also experienced the death of William's eight-year-old sister Anne in 1579. Deeply affected by her death, the family gave Anne a lavish funeral they most likely could not afford.

There are no records of William's life from 1579 until 1582. Some scholars believe that he taught school in another town and lived with family friends. Others speculate that he participated in secret political errands. He may simply have been working in the glove shop with his father.

WILLIAM AND ANNE

Sometime during this period, William began courting a woman named Anne Hathaway. She was from the village of Shottery, approximately two miles (3 km) through woods and farms from Stratford. The Hathaways were old friends of the Shakespeares. In the 1560s, John Shakespeare had

Maintaining Virtue

In *A Midsummer Night's Dream*, Hermia, a young girl, tells her lover that she must protect her virginity: "Nay, good Lysander, for my sake, my dear, / Lie further off yet; do not lie so near ... / Such separation may well be said / Becomes a virtuous bachelor and a maid, / So far be distant; and good night, sweet friend."[1]

helped Anne's father, Richard, pay off some of his debts. The Hathaways were neither nobility nor especially wealthy, but they had lived in Shottery for many generations and were respected and established farmers.

William Shakespeare never wrote anything about Anne, and their relationship was somewhat unusual. Anne was older than William by eight years. While it was not uncommon for an older man to court a younger woman, it was unusual for a man to court a woman who was so much older than himself. When William courted her, she was an independent woman, living on her own. When Anne's father, Richard Hathaway, died, he left his daughter a large annual income and property.

MARRIAGE

In late 1582, William and Anne found themselves in a tricky spot. Anne was pregnant. William was only 18 years old. The couple had only one choice. They arranged to be married—and quickly.

Generally, commoners were not strict about sexual behavior, and accidental pregnancies were not uncommon. However, pregnant women were expected to marry their lovers as soon as possible, without advertising the reason for their haste.

It did not really matter if they were in love or even wanted to be married to each other. During this time, love was not the usual reason for marriage. Marriage was a means of companionship and a way to produce heirs. Love was not a necessity. Anne and William were no exception.

In Elizabethan times, when a couple intended to marry, the vicar would publish the banns three weeks before the wedding date. The banns are a public announcement of a marriage. Each Sunday, the vicar would announce the proposed union in church, and the community could raise objections on legal or moral grounds. However, it was not unusual for a woman to be pregnant at the time of the wedding. It was even seen as a sign of good luck.

Nonetheless, William and Anne could not wait three weeks. Fortunately, they had another option.

Anne Whateley

The day before their marriage, William and Anne Hathaway applied for a marriage license. The clerk entered the names William Shakespeare and Anne Whateley into the record book. Some suspect that Shakespeare intended to marry her instead of Anne Hathaway. The most likely explanation is that the clerk made a mistake and entered the name of Whateley instead of Hathaway.

Two good friends of Anne's late father, Fulke Sandells and John Rychardson, posted a bond to speed up the banns. They paid the vicar and he agreed to announce the banns and marry the couple within a day. The banns of Anne Hathaway and William Shakespeare were published on November 30, 1582.

Most likely, William and Anne were married in the church at Temple Grafton, a parish near Anne's home of Shottery. The couple's friends and family would have attended the ceremony to witness the event and wish them well. According to the custom, the couple would have held hands during the ceremony to signify their bond. William likely placed the wedding ring on the fourth finger of Anne's left hand, the finger with the vein that supposedly ran straight to her heart. Anne's hair, according to custom, would have hung loose and unbraided around her shoulders.

The Wedding Register

Although the church near Shottery, in Temple Grafton, seems the most likely place for William and Anne to have been married, scholars have explored others. A nineteenth-century scholar went to the village of Luddington, which was three miles (5 km) outside of Temple Grafton. He searched unsuccessfully for the church register in which marriages, christenings, and funerals were recorded. Asking among the villagers, he was told that there had been a register once. However, on a cold day, the housekeeper in the vicar's house had burnt the document in order to heat her teakettle.

The new couple welcomed guests at the Hathaway home afterward for a bridal feast. There, William and Anne received gifts of gold, silver, and food. Six months later, baby Susanna was born. She was baptized on May 26, 1583. ⌐

William Shakespeare married Anne Hathaway in 1582.

London, 1574

THE START OF A
NEW LIFE

After Susanna's birth, William, Anne, and their daughter lived with John and Mary in the rambling Henley Street house. There are no records of Shakespeare's activities during this period, but it seems likely that it was a quiet time.

He most likely worked in the glove shop with his father and brothers. Anne gave birth again, this time to twins. The twins were baptized on February 2, 1585, and were named Judith and Hamnet. Anne and William named them after their close friends, Judith and Hamnet Sadler, who owned a bakery down the street. When the Sadlers' baby was born, they named him William.

THE LOST YEARS

During the period following the birth of Shakespeare's twins until the early 1590s, no records remain to indicate what Shakespeare was doing. Some have called this period "The Lost Years." All that is known with certainty is that at some point after 1585, the young Shakespeare left Stratford and his family behind and moved to London.

Some scholars have speculated that Shakespeare left Stratford because he

"Hate Away"

Scholars have found no writings of Shakespeare's either to or about his wife. Many believe that he did reference Anne Hathaway in a roundabout way in one of his sonnets. Sonnet 145 concludes with this couplet: "'I hate' from hate away she threw, / And sav'd my life, saying—'not you.'"[1]

"Hate away" could be a pun on "Hathaway." This sort of wordplay was common in Elizabethan plays and elsewhere in his work.

and Anne were unhappy. Shakespeare would go on to write many declarations of love in his plays, but in all of his years, he never dedicated a word of those to his wife or wrote any poems to her. For almost three decades, Shakespeare lived in London while Anne and his children remained in Stratford. Though he returned for visits, it is unclear how many times he actually returned home.

Beginning a Great Adventure

For whatever reason, Shakespeare left Stratford. Something enticed him, tugging him away from the quiet green banks of the Avon River. He packed a bundle with a few clothes, perhaps a cloak, and some bread and cheese for his journey. He checked his dagger in his waistband. Then he turned his back on the house and the town he had known since birth and stepped out onto the road to London.

It is unclear how Shakespeare left Stratford. He may have walked the road alone, with only the sound of his feet scuffling in the soft dirt and the birds in the hedges to fill his ears. Or he may have traveled with a group. Several acting troupes came to Stratford in the late 1580s. These players performed around the countryside until it was time to return to

William Shakespeare

London for their regular season in the playhouses. Shakespeare may have been accepted into one of these troupes as an apprentice. They would have continued traveling the countryside together with their costume wagon behind them.

London

When he arrived in London, Shakespeare would have found the city very different from Stratford. It was his first sight of the sprawling, bustling, colorful sixteenth-century city. Smoke hung over the city from thousands of cooking fires. At the entrance to London Bridge, the heads of traitors were impaled on spikes. Merchants jammed the streets selling a variety of meats, cheeses, spices, cloth, flowers, and other wares. Beggars moaned for alms, acrobats turned handsprings for coins, and balladeers strolled about singing their newest tunes.

For all of its excitement, London was a terribly dirty place. Without modern plumbing and waste disposal systems, people could not take regular baths, and the city reeked of waste and rotting garbage. Sewers emptied directly into the Thames River. Everywhere, rats scurried through the piles of trash, digging and burrowing and crawling with fleas.

• 43 •

Shakespeare and his friends sometimes visited the Falcon Tavern.

London was also a magical place. It was full of color—wealthy people wore elaborate silk capes and dresses. People danced, played musical instruments, performed elaborate gymnastics, and sang comic songs. Every week, people jammed the great playhouses—the Theatre, the Curtain, the Rose, the Red Bull, the Swan, and the Fortune—to see the newest plays.

THE THEATERS AND THE PLAYS

Shakespeare had probably never seen a real playhouse before he came to London. In Stratford and other country villages, the players performed wherever they could—in inns, in the homes of wealthy patrons, and occasionally outside in the open.

For the most part, theaters were round with an elevated stage projecting out into a large, bare yard. There was no ceiling—only the sky overhead. Galleries with seats circled the walls on two or three levels. There was usually a trapdoor in the floor of the stage for theatrical effects and two doors at the back for stage entrances and exits.

The Talents of an Actor

Shakespeare acted in the plays he wrote. In addition to their memorization and speaking skills, actors had to execute elaborate stage fights with different weapons, do acrobatics, perform complex dances, and play several musical instruments.

For a pence, peasants could stand in the crowded yard. They were called "groundlings" in theater slang. Two pence bought a seat in the galleries, and three pence let a patron sit under the wall overhang, out of the way of the rain and sun. The stage was bare. Sets were not used at this time—perhaps a chair or a pedestal, but nothing else. The costumes were elaborate and magnificent and included silks, embroidery, massive skirts, capes, doublets, decorated hats, hosiery, and slippers.

Marlowe's *Tamburlaine*

Christopher Marlowe wrote *Tamburlaine* in 1587 and 1588. The story follows the conquests of the title character, Tamburlaine, as he conquers distant people, goes back on promises, and even kills his own son in search of achieving greatness.

Audiences loved the play, and it was a huge success. Most notably, *Tamburlaine* is a diversion from the awkward language and loose plots of earlier plays. Many Elizabethan playwrights modeled their work on *Tamburlaine*. Its blank verse style became standard for many dramatists.

Shakespeare's first set of plays, written in the late 1580s, was the *Henry VI* trilogy. Scholars speculate that Shakespeare may have joined the Queen's Men, a rival troupe of Marlowe's. They asked Shakespeare to write something to compete with *Tamburlaine*. Shakespeare's *Henry VI* responds to parts of *Tamburlaine*. While Marlowe's *Tamburlaine* achieves conquest and success because of his ruthlessness, Shakespeare's characters are just as ruthless, but seem disturbed and incapable of achieving greatness.

TAMBURLAINE

Queen Elizabeth I loved the theater. Under

her patronage, London theater flourished. She regularly ordered new plays by Shakespeare and his peers to be performed at her court. Queen Elizabeth was a flamboyant, artistic person who had a lifelong love of music, dance, and drama.

Christopher Marlowe was one of the most popular playwrights in London. Marlowe was Shakespeare's age, but by the late 1580s he had already written several very popular plays. He was a charismatic and brilliant dramatist. In 1587, London theatergoers poured into the Rose to see Marlowe's new work, *Tamburlaine*. The role of the title character, Tamburlaine, was played by Edward Alleyn. At the age of 21, Alleyn was already one of the leading actors in London.

It is not certain that Shakespeare saw the performance of *Tamburlaine* with Alleyn in the lead, but it is very likely. The play, which details the

Gender on Stage

All of the actors in Shakespeare's time were men. Women were not allowed on stage. Young boys performed the female roles until their voices changed. Scholar Russ McDonald speculates that from 1605 through 1608, Shakespeare's company had a brilliant boy actor. During those years, Shakespeare wrote some of his greatest female roles, such as Lady Macbeth.

conquests of Tamburlaine, is notable for its use of blank verse. Marlowe's powerful words would have had a strong effect on the young Shakespeare. Shortly after the success of *Tamburlaine*, Shakespeare began to write words of his own.

At some point in the late 1580s and early 1590s, the crowds that had gasped and wept at Marlowe's plays were treated for the first time to the plays of William Shakespeare.

Edward Alleyn played the lead in Tamburlaine.

Richard III *was among Shakespeare's earliest plays.*

Leaving His Mark on London

fter Shakespeare arrived in London, he became acquainted with a group of young playwrights, poets, and writers: Christopher Marlowe, Thomas Watson, Thomas Nashe, and Robert Greene. These men called themselves "university wits"—meaning they had all gone to university. They were considered some of the brightest young talents in London.

Shakespeare would know these men for the rest of their lives. He may have collaborated on work with some, especially Thomas Nashe. But there may have been tension between William and his new friends— Shakespeare had not attended university and the others had.

THE FRUIT OF HIS LABORS

Shakespeare wrote a lot during this time. In the late 1580s and early 1590s, Shakespeare averaged about two plays a year, in addition to sonnets and poems. He would continue to write at this pace until the end of his life. Though the exact order in which the plays were written is not known, many of Shakespeare's most famous plays were written during this period. He wrote the

Renaissance

Shakespeare had entered London during a renaissance period of theater and literary arts. This period was a surge in creative thinking. There was more attention to plays and literature than there had been in the medieval period. This renaissance was also due to the support of a theater-loving queen who allowed a group of extraordinary young writers to release their creativity in an outpouring of art.

bloody and violent *Titus Andronicus* and the romantic *Romeo and Juliet.* He also wrote *Richard III*, *The Taming of the Shrew*, and *Love's Labour's Lost*.

In the summer of 1592, Shakespeare may have been writing for and playing with a troupe called the Earl of Pembroke's Men. There is some evidence that this troupe played some of the earliest performances of Shakespeare's *Henry VI*. It is also possible that he was writing for a number of troupes. During this time, an outbreak of bubonic plague spread through the city. Though little was known about the disease, Elizabethans were aware that plague spread more quickly among crowds of people. When the number of deaths due to the plague began to rise, the Privy Council would order public gathering spaces such as bearbaiting arenas, taverns, and playhouses to be shut down. The summer of 1592 was one of those times.

Titus Andronicus

Titus Andronicus is one of Shakespeare's earliest tragedies. It is also one of his most bloody and violent. It is so violent that some scholars have speculated that Shakespeare did not write all of it himself—some lines are similar to the writing of his friend George Peele. Much of the gore centers around Lavinia, Titus's daughter. One stage direction instructs her to enter with her hands cut off, her tongue cut out, and "ravished" [raped]. Later in the play, Lavinia writes the names of her attackers in the dirt by holding a stick between the stumps of her hands.

Shakespeare's plays were often performed for Queen Elizabeth I.

If Shakespeare was playing with a regular troupe, they probably packed up and left the plague-ridden city to tour the countryside. If Shakespeare stayed in London, he would have needed money. The closure of the theaters meant no more performances of his plays. According to some scholars, it was during these years when a new opportunity arose for Shakespeare.

Shakespeare is shown lifting a cap, a symbol of fame, from Francis Bacon.

Love and Poetry

In 1593 and 1594, Shakespeare published two long poems he had written on commission: *Venus and Adonis* and *The Rape of Lucrece*. *Venus and Adonis* is Shakespeare's first work to appear in print under his name. Shakespeare dedicated these poems to a nobleman named Henry Wriothesley, the third Earl of Southampton. Wriothesley was a handsome youth who was a noted patron of the theater. It is likely he was Shakespeare's patron.

During this period, Shakespeare wrote some of his famous sonnets. Scholars have speculated on why Shakespeare wrote these sonnets and for whom they were written. In many of the poems, the speaker is expressing a passionate, romantic love for a beautiful young man. The young man's identity is not given, but many scholars have speculated that the young man is the Earl of Southampton, who was known for his feminine beauty. Others believe a young nobleman, the Earl of Pembroke, is the youth in the poems. Some even believe that Shakespeare had a love affair with this mysterious youth. Others speculate that Shakespeare was cleverly making fun

The Dark Lady

Shakespeare makes reference to a "dark lady" in some of his sonnets. Scholars have speculated that Shakespeare may have written these about a woman with whom he was having an affair or loved from a distance. However, because the sonnets are works of fiction, others have pointed out that the narrator of the poems is not necessarily Shakespeare.

Shakespeare may also have been making fun of other poets who always wrote sonnets about women who looked like goddesses.

of the popular aristocratic pastime of writing stuffy sonnets to exaggeratedly beautiful ladies.

CRITICISM

By the early 1590s, William Shakespeare was known around town as the young poet who rivaled Christopher Marlowe. Audiences flocked to the theaters when Shakespeare's new plays were performed. His fame annoyed some of the more educated playwrights, or "university wits"—in particular, Robert Greene.

Greene was a flamboyant, brilliant man with fiery red hair. He held two master's degrees and was considered a gifted poet and writer. Greene also had an extraordinary appetite and consumed large amounts of alcohol.

The young Shakespeare irritated him immensely. Greene may have thought it was absurd of Shakespeare to come into their group without a university education and consider himself their equal. One night, Greene ate too much pickled herring and drank too much wine. He fell very ill. While on his deathbed, Greene called for ink and paper. He wrote a long, nasty declaration against his fellow poets—in particular, William Shakespeare.

After Greene's death, in 1592, a printer named Henry Chettle published the piece in a pamphlet called *Greene's Groats-Worth of Wit*. In it, Greene called Shakespeare an intruder, an inexperienced novice masquerading as an expert, uneducated, and a plagiarist.

Shakespeare was furious at these insults and contacted the publisher. Soon afterward, Chettle published an apology in which he insisted that he had nothing whatsoever to do with the content of the pamphlet.

Greene's Groats-Worth of Wit

The first record of Shakespeare's presence in London is in Robert Greene's 1592 pamphlet. From this mention, scholars know two things: Shakespeare was in London, and his success as a playwright made others jealous. Greene is vehement in his accusations. Following is an excerpt from the pamphlet:

Yes trust them not: for there is an upstart Crow, beautified with our feathers, that with his Tiger's heart wrapped in a Player's hide, supposes he is as well able to bombast out a blank verse as the best of you: and being an absolute Johannes Factotum, is in his own conceit the only Shakescene in the country.[1]

Greene accuses Shakespeare not only of being an arrogant newcomer (the "upstart Crow") but also of being an actor as well as a playwright. The university wits thought that playwrights were of a higher status than actors. Greene believed Shakespeare was insulting the other playwrights by mixing the two professions. That is what Greene meant when he referred to Shakespeare as a "Johannes Factotum"—a jack-of-all-trades. The line "Tiger's heart wrapped in a Player's hide" is a direct reference to a line in Shakespeare's *Henry VI*, in which a character refers to a tiger's heart wrapped in a woman's hide.

Chettle's Apology

Chettle realized the mistake he made by printing Greene's pamphlet. In his apology, he noted, "How I have all the time of my conversing in printing hindered the bitter inveighing against scholars, it hath been very well known; and how in that I dealt I can sufficiently prove ... [I] might have used my own discretion [in printing the pamphlet] ... that I did not, I am as sorry, as if the original fault has been my fault ..."[2]

The incident soon passed. By this time, Shakespeare was 30 years old and all of his major rivals were gone. Greene was dead. Thomas Watson had died of illness, probably the plague. Marlowe had been stabbed in a tavern fight in 1593. The next generation of playwrights, including Ben Jonson and John Webster, would not produce serious work for almost 20 years. Shakespeare was entering his prime, and great times were ahead.

ℋ
PLEASANT
Conceited Comedie
CALLED,
Loues labors loſt.

As it vvas preſented before her Highnes
this laſt Chriſtmas.

Newly correcſted and augmented
By W. Shakeſpere

Imprinted at London by *W.W.*
for *Cutbert Burby*.
1598.

The title page of Love's Labour's Lost *is the earliest published page
containing Shakespeare's name.*

Outbreaks of plague swept through Europe during the late 1500s.

HAMNET AND *CAESAR*

he year 1594 was difficult for many players,
but for Shakespeare, it proved favorable.
Plague swept London again, and the theaters closed.
Patrons and players died from the plague. Many
of the leading troupes went bankrupt for lack of

performances. They sold off their costumes and playbooks to pay their debts. The best players in London soon joined together in two troupes: the Lord Admiral's Men and the Lord Chamberlain's Men. The Lord Admiral's Men included the great actor, Edward Alleyn. The Lord Chamberlain's Men boasted Richard Burbage, Alleyn's rival, and London's great comic actor, Will Kempe. It also had William Shakespeare.

In the Lord Chamberlain's Men, Shakespeare found his theatrical home. He remained with the troupe until his retirement and wrote some of his greatest works: *King Lear*, *Othello*, *Hamlet*, and *Macbeth*. Shakespeare had more than an artistic attachment to the troupe though. Along with Burbage, Kempe, and others, he had bought a share of the group. He was a part-owner and entitled to a share of the profits. This proved to be a wise investment. His income from the

Edward Alleyn

Edward Alleyn was one of the leading actors of London. He was unusually tall for the time—over six feet (1.8 m)—and possessed a booming voice and charismatic stage presence. Both Christopher Marlowe and Shakespeare wrote some of their greatest leading roles for him.

Lord Chamberlain's Men would help Shakespeare become wealthy.

Seasons passed. Shakespeare wrote *Richard II*. He acted, wrote, and pored over the group's finances with James, Richard, and Cuthbert Burbage. The troupe was invited to play at the royal court. Around 1595, Shakespeare wrote *A Midsummer Night's Dream*. The magical romance may have been performed at a noble wedding. The glove maker's son, who had never gone to university, was becoming rich.

NEWS FROM HOME

In 1596, a messenger arrived from Stratford bearing news.

The Bubonic Plague

Bubonic plague is a devastating disease that had a major impact on the populations of Europe and Asia during medieval times. In the fourteenth century, 200 years before Shakespeare's birth, Europe experienced the Black Death. This massive epidemic of bubonic plague wiped out approximately one-third of the European population in three years. Smaller outbreaks continued to sweep Europe and England until the sixteenth century.

Plague is spread by infected rats and fleas. Humans contract the disease when they are bitten by a contaminated animal. People did not figure out how it was transmitted until the end of the nineteenth century.

Plague symptoms generally appear three to eight days after a person has been infected. They experience chills, fever, diarrhea, and the telltale swelling of the lymph nodes—buboes. Before modern medical treatment, the plague killed up to 90 percent of those infected. Poor nutrition and unsanitary living conditions added to the mortality rate. Today, plague is rarely contracted, but it is easily treated with antibiotics.

Hamnet, Shakespeare's 11-year-old son, was gravely ill. Typhus and dysentery had swept through Stratford that year. By August, Hamnet was dead. He was buried at Holy Trinity Church in Stratford on August 11, 1596. Although there is no record, Shakespeare would probably have wanted to return home for the funeral.

After Hamnet's death Shakespeare purchased a handsome house in Stratford in 1597 and moved his family into it. New Place, as it was called, was one of the nicest houses in town. The house was three stories of brick and timber. It had five gables and ten rooms, each with its own fireplace. There were gardens, orchards, and two barns. It was a dwelling fit for a gentleman's family. Perhaps Robert Greene's remark about the uneducated "upstart Crow" stuck somewhere in the poet's mind—this was not a house for a mere actor.

Scholars have also been unable to find any references to his son's death in his work. In the years following his son's death, he wrote some of his lightest comedies: *The Merry Wives of Windsor, As You Like It,* and *Much Ado About Nothing.* His amazing output—two plays a year—remained constant.

Trouble in London

When William Shakespeare returned to London, he was one of the most famous playwrights in the city. He was also a savvy businessman who was steadily accumulating wealth and property. The London crowds mobbed the theaters whenever one of his plays was featured, and he had written two a year for the past decade. His words could reduce audiences to tears or provoke uproarious laughter. Still, despite all of this, he was troubled by a problem with his troupe's lease.

Shakespeare was in his mid-thirties. He was the playwright and an actor for his theater troupe, the Lord Chamberlain's Men, which was one of the best in the city. They could command full audiences every night at their playhouse, the Theatre, due to Shakespeare's brilliant plays and the antics of the famous comic actor, Will Kempe.

Successful as they were, the Lord Chamberlain's Men did not own the land on which the Theatre stood.

Bear Baiting

It is unclear what Giles Allen wanted to do with the Theatre after the lease of the Lord Chamberlain's Men expired. One common alternate use for playhouses was the popular, brutal entertainment of bear baiting. In this blood sport, trained dogs would attack a chained bear. The animals would fight to the death. Sometimes, the bear would break loose and run through the crowd.

A performance of Shakespeare's A Midsummer Night's Dream

The business leader of the troupe, James Burbage, had rented it from Giles Allen since 1576. The lease was up in April 1597, and Allen wanted to raise the rent from 14 pounds a year to 24. This was a huge amount of money, but the men were fond of the Theatre and they needed a home stage.

Printing

Shakespeare's scripts for his plays were hand-written. Each actor's copy had to be carefully copied. At the time, it was not practical to typeset manuscripts for only a few people.

Burbage reluctantly agreed to the increased rent. In addition, Allen told Burbage the troupe could only use the Theatre for five more years. The troupe would have to find a new location to perform. Burbage, probably with the help of his partner, Shakespeare, started looking for a new site. Unfortunately, in January 1597, Burbage died. He passed his position in the troupe onto his sons, Richard and Cuthbert, who were now in charge of the finances.

The Lord Chamberlain's Men found themselves in a state of crisis. But the sons had no more success than their father in negotiating an acceptable lease with Allen. In April, Allen agreed to allow the actors to stay at the Theatre for a few additional months, but the need to find a new home was dire. If they could not find a permanent place to stay, Shakespeare feared, the troupe would have to break up.

A Second Crisis

In July of 1597, a rival acting troupe, the Earl of Pembroke's Men, put on a new work by the young playwright Ben Jonson. *The Isle of Dogs* featured sharp satire of various members of the current London administration. The audience loved it, but the authorities were furious. With that, the Privy Council, Queen Elizabeth's closest advisors, ordered all the playhouses in London temporarily shut down, including the Theatre.

Luckily, the shutdown was temporary. Within a few months, the theaters reopened. But Shakespeare's actors still had no permanent home. They tried playing at the nearby Curtain theater, but that building was falling apart. The attendance started dropping off and Allen refused to budge on the matter of the lease of the Theatre.

The troupe needed a home. They also needed cash. Shakespeare and the Burbages arranged to do something they usually tried to avoid—they sold off four of

Ben Jonson

During his time in London, Shakespeare moved in a circle of young playwrights and poets who regularly collaborated and competed for audiences and patrons. One of these was Ben Jonson.

Jonson wrote numerous plays and lyric poems. He and Thomas Nashe co-wrote *Isle of Dogs*. Nashe was also a member of Shakespeare's circle. *Isle of Dogs* provoked outrage among the London authorities when it was performed in the summer of 1597. No copies of the play survive, but it is thought to have poked fun at Queen Elizabeth and her Privy Council. Jonson, who also acted in the play, was arrested along with two other players and imprisoned. Nashe's home was raided. Luckily, the incident soon died down and Jonson was released by October 1597.

Shakespeare's plays. These plays had been written specifically for the company: *Richard III*, *Richard II*, *Henry IV, Part One*, and *Love's Labour's Lost*.

Then, Shakespeare and the Burbages came up with a brilliant solution. In reading over the terms of their lease, one of them had noticed that Allen only owned the land on which the Theatre stood, not the structure itself. The lease stated that the building belonged to Richard and Cuthbert. A plan was hatched.

The men located and rented a piece of land across the Thames River, in the neighborhood of Southwark. It was near an existing theater, the Rose. According to the new lease, the troupe could move in on Christmas Day. There was just one problem: there was no building on the land.

THE
Tragicall Hiſtorie of
HAMLET,
Prince of Denmarke.

By William Shakeſpeare.

Newly imprinted and enlarged to almoſt as much
againe as it was, according to the true and perfect
Coppie.

AT LONDON,
Printed by I. R. for N. L. and are to be ſold at his
ſhoppe vnder Saint Dunſtons Church in
Fleeſtreet. 1605.

Hamlet *is one of Shakespeare's most famous plays.*

The Globe Theatre at Southwark, London

THE NEW GLOBE THEATRE

he night of December 28, 1598, was frigid. London was in the midst of a cold snap. In the darkness, figures carrying torches gathered near the Theatre. They carried axes, shovels, picks, and swords. The Lord Chamberlain's Men had gathered to dismantle their playhouse while Allen was in the country on his Christmas holiday.

Armed guards were stationed around the perimeter to ward off the small crowd of onlookers that had gathered. By the light of the torches and with the Burbages directing the operation, the actors and hired workmen started to take the Theatre apart. The men worked into the morning. The timbers were loaded onto sleds and wagons and transported across the river.

Allen returned from the country to find the playhouse reduced to a pile of boards and rubble. He was furious. The workers refused to stop when asked.

His rantings were of no avail. Within four days, the Theatre had been entirely disassembled, carted across the Thames, and laid out on the new site. A talented carpenter, Peter Streete, fit the pieces together and constructed new ones. The new building was going to be better than the old.

Giles Allen's Fury

Giles Allen was livid at the dismantling of the Theatre. Allen described what he saw that night, "[The crew] then therein with great violence, [not] only then and there forcibly and riotously resisting your subjects, servants and farmers, but also then and there pulling, breaking and throwing down the said Theatre in a very outrageous, violent and riotous sort, to the great disturbance and terrifying [not] only of your subjects ... but of divers others of your Majesty's loving subjects there near inhabiting."[1]

Building the Globe

Over the next few months, the new theater took
shape. Shakespeare and the Burbages had told
Streete what they wanted: the round shape typical
of Elizabethan theaters, but with three galleries and
the stage jutting out into the central courtyard. The
playhouse was magnificent when it was finished. The
stage was 50 feet (15 m) across, and there was room
for approximately 3,000 patrons in the galleries and
courtyard.

All of this cost the troupe a great deal of money;
their finances had to be refigured. A small group
of men functioned as investors: the Burbages,
Shakespeare, and four of the main
actors. These four actors were
John Heminges, Thomas Pope,
Augustine Philips, and Will Kempe.
Shakespeare had a one-tenth share in
the new playhouse, as well as a one-
tenth share in the company and the
revenue it brought in. In addition to
his share in the troupe, his share in
the building entitled him to part of
the income from renting the building
for other uses.

The Modern Globe

A replica of Shakespeare's
Globe Theatre was built
in London, only 200
yards (182 m) from the
site of the original Globe.
Built in 1997 by Sam
Wanamaker, it is a near-
exact copy of the original
theater. It even includes a
thatched roof—the only
one in London.

A reconstruction of Shakespeare's Globe Theatre

By June 1599, the new theater was completed. It was round, like the world, and the company named it the Globe. Its motto was *Totus mundus agit histrionem* (all the world's a stage). Some of the most famous plays in the history of the western English-speaking world, written by their own William Shakespeare, would be performed at the Globe Theatre.

Will Kempe was the resident comic actor with the Lord Chamberlain's Men. Kempe was known for his dancing and songs and was immensely popular with audiences. Shortly after the move, Kempe had a falling-out with the other actors. He sold his share and left. The first play Shakespeare wrote after Kempe's departure, *Julius Caesar*, had no part for a comic actor; the company had not yet found a replacement.

The Lord Chamberlain's Men

The Lord Chamberlain's Men was founded in 1594 under the patronage of Henry Carey, First Baron Hudson, and the then Lord Chamberlain. The Lord Chamberlain is an officer of the Royal Household and is a member of the Privy Council.

The company thrived under the management of Richard Burbage. A core of six to eight members split the company's profits and debts. In addition to the shareholders, the company hired additional men to act in the plays. After awhile, some of these men became shareholders as well. The company's most popular members were playwright William Shakespeare and the comic actor Will Kempe, although Kempe would eventually leave the troupe.

The Lord Chamberlain's Men played in various rented spaces before they built the Globe Theatre and acquired the Blackfriars Theatre. In 1603, the company became known as the King's Men under the patronage of King James I.

Later, two young actors, Henry Condell and John Heminges, joined the company. They are credited with compiling and editing Shakespeare's plays.

AT THE GLOBE

The new Globe Theatre was a brilliant sight. The pillars supporting the overhang were painted in bright blues, reds, and golds. The empty galleries would soon be filled with audience members ready to see what Shakespeare had in store for them.

One day in June of 1599, around two o'clock in the afternoon, the gates of the new Globe Theatre opened. The crowd of peasants pushed into the yard. Wealthy yeomen and nobles took their seats in the galleries. Vendors strolled the crowds, hawking oranges, apples, gingerbread, and beer. The voices of the audience would have reached the ears of the actors backstage as they prepared to make their entrances.

"Hence! Home, you idle creatures, get you home,"[2] ordered the bureaucrat Flavius as he stepped out onto the stage. *Julius Caesar*, Shakespeare's first play for the new theater, had begun. *Julius Caesar* was a great success. Shakespeare once again proved his talent. For the first time, his name began appearing on copies of his plays when they were printed, in hopes of attracting more buyers.

An Eyewitness Account

On September 21, 1599, a Swiss gentleman named Thomas Platter visited London. He wrote to his friends back home that he had seen a production of *Julius Caesar* at the Globe. His description is one of the few eyewitness accounts of Shakespeare's plays. Platter wrote, "[After] dinner, at about two o'clock, I went with my party across the water; in the straw-thatched house we saw the tragedy of the first Emperor Julius Caesar, very pleasantly performed, with approximately fifteen characters ..."[3]

Although he was successful, Shakespeare was worried. In 1599, two new troupes began playing in nearby neighborhoods. Two troupes, the Children of Paul and the Children of the Chapel at Blackfriars, were very good and attracted massive audiences. Even though the actors were all boys, their talent attracted a large audience. The Lord Chamberlain's Men needed to keep their edge—the work must not be allowed to slip. Shakespeare may have thought they needed something even better than *Caesar*—something different. ⌐

Borrowing and Copying

Most of Shakespeare's plays were updates of older plays or rewrites of plays his friends had written. This was common among playwrights at the time. They also seldom signed their work. They all copied lines from each other—in some cases, borrowing entire speeches or characters. Shakespeare also incorporated many of Christopher Marlowe's stylistic elements into his own work. Today, this would be considered plagiarism, but in Shakespeare's time authors had a different view of work ownership.

A sketch depicting the comic actor Will Kempe

Act 1 of Hamlet

MAKING HIS MARK

Shakespeare's inspiration for his works came from the world around him. Pieces of interesting news, interactions between friends, historical events, and pieces of old tales all served to inspire him. Scholars look for links between

Shakespeare's life and his writing, but this has not been easy. Most of the time, what Shakespeare was writing does not parallel what was happening in his own life.

Sometime between 1601 and 1603, Shakespeare wrote one of his greatest works—perhaps, his masterpiece—*Hamlet.* The heart-wrenching story of a young prince became known as more serious, profound, and tragic than any he had written before. Shakespeare's father was dying during these years; it is possible the poet was grappling with thoughts of mortality.

The country was also in the midst of a worrisome period. Queen Elizabeth was nearing the end of her life, yet the childless queen refused to name a successor. Many feared the country would descend into civil war upon her death. Shakespeare may have written *Hamlet*, with its themes of succession and betrayal after the death of a king, to reflect the mood of his audience.

Interestingly, Shakespeare wrote *Hamlet* during one of the most prosperous, successful times in

Hamlet

Hamlet is Shakespeare's longest play. In its entirety, it runs over four-and-a-half hours. The first recorded performance was in 1601. It was the only one of Shakespeare's plays to be performed at the universities of Oxford and Cambridge.

Around 1604, Shakespeare lived with the Mountjoy family. Christopher Mountjoy was a wigmaker. While Shakespeare was there, he helped to arrange a marriage between the Mountjoy daughter and one of the apprentices, a boy named Stephen Belott. Years later, Belott wanted to sue his father-in-law for failing to pay the entire dowry that was promised. Shakespeare was called as a witness to testify in court but said he could remember few details.

his life. He was at the height of his fame at the turn of the century. He was admired and respected. He was financially comfortable, settled, and bursting with creativity.

As with many of Shakespeare's plays, the story of the Danish prince Hamlet is not original. Shakespeare based *Hamlet* on a play written years earlier by Thomas Kyd. Kyd's play, referred to as the *Ur-Hamlet*, has been lost. No one knows how much of Kyd's play Shakespeare incorporated into his own version of *Hamlet*.

Hamlet represented a turning point for Shakespeare. Before this play, Shakespeare had mostly written light comedies and history plays. Now, he began writing serious, complex tragedies such as *Othello*, *King Lear*, and *Macbeth*. Many scholars consider these plays his greatest works—and he wrote them all in the years immediately following *Hamlet*.

The tragedies proved to be a success and crowds continued to pack the Globe whenever a new play was offered. With the money he earned from these performances, Shakespeare bought land in Stratford. He was an experienced businessman and gained a reputation as a fair landlord.

THE QUEEN IS DEAD, LONG LIVE THE KING!

In 1603, Queen Elizabeth I was dying. For two days, she remained standing, refusing to lie down for fear she would never get up again. Finally, she was convinced to lie in her bed. She had ruled her country for 45 years, seeing it through times of peace and strife. The coronation ring, which

Famous Monologue

Shakespeare's most famous monologue is from *Hamlet*. In the following excerpt, Hamlet considers the possibility of suicide. Ultimately, he decides that it is best to go on living:

To be, or not to be: that is the question

Whether 'tis nobler in the mind to suffer

The slings and arrows of outrageous fortune,

Or to take arms against a sea of troubles,

And by opposing end them? To die: to sleep;

No more; and by a sleep to say we end

The heart-ache and the thousand natural shocks

That flesh is heir to, 'tis a consummation

Devoutly to be wish'd. To die, to sleep;

To sleep: perchance to dream: ay, there's the rub;

For in that sleep of death what dreams may come

When we have shuffled off this mortal coil,

Must give us pause: there's the respect

That makes calamity of so long life;...[1]

symbolized her marriage to England, had sunk so deeply into her flesh that it had to be sawed from her finger. Elizabeth I had never married and had no children. Until this moment, she had refused to name her heir. Finally, she indicated that James VI, the King of Scotland, would succeed her as James I of England. On March 24, 1603, Queen Elizabeth died. At the end of her reign, England was one of the most wealthy and powerful countries in the world.

Messengers galloped on horseback through the night to Edinburgh, Scotland. When they arrived, they dropped to their knees at the feet of their new king. "The Queen is dead, long live the King!" echoed in the night air. The coronation ring was placed in James's hand. The crown had passed peacefully.

King James I loved dancing, music, and plays even more than Elizabeth. Six days after he arrived at

The Actor

When Shakespeare acted in the plays he wrote, evidence suggests he typically played the roles of older gentlemen. Notable roles included: Adam in *As You Like It*, the Ghost in *Hamlet*, and kings in history plays such as *Henry IV, Part One*.

King James I

his palace, James summoned the best theater troupe
in the city to his side—the Lord Chamberlain's
Men, with William Shakespeare. James declared the
troupe was now under his patronage and would be

hereafter known as the King's Men. Shakespeare was now more than a successful playwright and actor, he was an employee of the king.

Theater in London blossomed under James I. During Elizabeth's reign, the Lord Chamberlain's Men played at court about three times a year. King James requested their performances 14 times a year, and he always attended the performances. During the winter of 1603–1604, the King's Men performed eight plays, seven of which were written by Shakespeare. The king's favorite was *The Merchant of Venice*—he ordered it performed twice in three days.

The King's Men was an influential group. In 1608, the troupe used some of its power in a new business venture. Years earlier, Richard Burbage's father, James, had bought a large section of London property that included the Blackfriars theater. For years, troupes of children had

Children's Troupes

Before the King's Men began playing at Blackfriars, an acting troupe made up of young boys, called the Children of the Chapel Royal, played at that theater. They and other all-boy troupes were popular in Shakespeare's day. They performed complicated, full-length dramas, including those of the Greek and Roman poets. The Elizabethans thought that the boys represented a "pure" form of theater since they were innocent youngsters.

performed there, but now the theater was empty. James Burbage had wanted work done on the hall so that it could be opened as London's first enclosed, roofed theater. But the neighbors objected and raised a petition against the plan.

A New Life at Blackfriars

Richard Burbage and the other shareholders of the King's Men, including Shakespeare, saw that they could revitalize James Burbage's plan. This time, no one dared fight the powerful troupe backed by the king. In 1608, the company put on its first play at Blackfriars. Now the troupe had two theaters.

Blackfriars was a different enterprise than the Globe. It was much smaller, holding only 500 audience members to the Globe's 3,000. At Blackfriars, everyone had a seat. It was also more expensive, at two shillings as opposed to a few pence at the Globe. The higher price did not matter, because the Blackfriars' audiences included the wealthy gentry and aristocracy.

The smaller space and the full roof enabled the actors to put on plays that were more intimate. Shakespeare began writing romances such as *Cymbeline, Pericles, Winter's Tale*, and *The Tempest*. These plays used a more quiet dialogue and soft movement, rather than the booming speeches and broad comedy that played so well in the Globe. Blackfriars could also be lit by candlelight, so the King's Men began putting on evening performances. The players would garb themselves in gauzy, fluttering fabrics and gilt that showed up well under the flickering flames of the candles and torches.

Not all of the changes at Blackfriars were in stagecraft. The rich patrons wanted to come to the playhouse to be seen, not just to see. For a fee, nobles were allowed to sit on the stage during the play, so that everyone could admire their beautiful clothes. The nobles could get up and walk about while the play was going on. Although it helped increase their earnings, this likely annoyed the actors. As for Shakespeare, he was growing older and turning his eyes toward retirement. ⌐

Richard Burbage

Shakespeare is shown reading to his family.

A FINAL BOW

On June 29, 1613, the King's Men were ready to perform William Shakespeare's new play, *Henry VIII*, at the Globe Theatre. Crowds streamed into the playhouse, excited for the new play.

The play began. Everything was going as practiced. Then, disaster struck. As part of the action, a cannon fired. This was a common piece of stagecraft, but this time, the cannon misfired. A piece of cloth caught fire as it flew from the cannon. It soared above the heads of the audience and struck the dry straw thatch of the Globe's roof. The roof quickly caught fire, spreading rapidly. People panicked and rushed toward the door. Pieces of burning thatch fell from the ceiling and landed on the audience. One man's pants caught fire and he put the flames out by pouring a bottle of ale on himself.

Within just a few minutes, it was over. The Globe had burned to the ground. The magnificent wood and thatch theater, where so many of Shakespeare's greatest works had been performed, was now nothing more than smoldering ashes and timbers spread across the ground.

SOLITUDE IN STRATFORD

Shakespeare was not at that performance to witness the destruction of the theater he had built. Presumably, the news of the fire reached Shakespeare through one of his friends. Shakespeare had returned to Stratford when he had retired in 1611. He had left London for a quieter life in Stratford. He may have been ill or tired of the rapid pace of the London theater business. Perhaps he just missed spending time with his family. For the first time in more than two decades, Shakespeare was living with his family in New Place, the home he had bought in 1597. Judith was still unmarried, but Susanna had wed a man named John Hall a few years earlier.

The years in Stratford were quiet. Shakespeare was still writing. He occasionally returned to London to work on plays. He collaborated with John Fletcher, a young playwright and member of the King's Men. Fletcher worked with Shakespeare on *Henry VIII, The Two Noble Kinsmen,* and *Cardenio*, a play which has been lost.

Susanna had given birth to a baby, Elizabeth. His daughter Judith married Thomas Quiney, a local

John Fletcher

John Fletcher was already known as a playwright by the time he worked with Shakespeare on *Henry VIII, The Two Noble Kinsmen,* and *Cardenio*. After Shakespeare died, Fletcher took over as resident playwright for the King's Men. He held that position until he died of plague at the age of 46.

New Place in Stratford, England

vintner, or wine seller, in February 1616. A month after his marriage to Judith, Quiney was ordered to appear in court. He had fathered a child with a local woman who died in childbirth.

Shakespeare was most likely very weak at this point. On March 25, 1616, the day before Quiney was set to appear in court, Shakespeare called a lawyer to his bedside. Shakespeare was a rich man, and he was determined that Quiney would not get any of his wealth. He ordered the attorney to alter his will. New Place and all of his land, livestock, and money was to go to Susanna. Judith was to receive only a small sum as an allowance with the restriction that it should only be given to her, not Quiney.

The Last Word

Anne Hathaway was alive and well during her husband's decline. She and William had been married for more than 30 years. They had lived together barely a decade. Anne received almost nothing in her husband's will—no money, no land, not even the house she lived in. All of that went to Susanna. A widow's portion of Shakespeare's money would have been given to Anne by law. It would not have been needed to be

Shakespeare's Will

Though the bulk of his estate went to Susanna and her husband, Shakespeare left a few tokens to other people. He left his sword to his friend Thomas Combe and money to buy remembrance rings for three of his fellow players, including Richard Burbage. To Judith, in addition to her small allowance, he left a silver and gilt bowl.

mentioned in the will. In his will, Shakespeare wrote this line concerning Anne: "Item I give unto my wife my second best bed with the furniture."[1] Some scholars believe this inheritance reflected an unhappy marriage. Others have argued that the second-best bed was the marital bed and this was an appropriate bequest from a husband to a wife.

A month later, on April 23, 1616, Shakespeare died. He was 52 years old. William Shakespeare was buried on April 25, 1616, at Holy Trinity Church, near his son,

Susanna and Judith

Susanna Shakespeare was William and Anne's oldest child. Susanna was probably a devoted Catholic, which was a crime during the reign of Queen Elizabeth. In 1606, she refused to take communion at Easter and was listed as a "recusant"—a secret Catholic.

In 1613, after her marriage, she was accused by a local man, John Lane, of adultery with another man, Rafe Smith. Susanna brought a case against Lane for slander and won in court. Smith was excommunicated.

Scholars speculate that Susanna might have inherited some of her father's talents as a writer. The inscription on her gravestone read in part,

Witty above her sex, but that's not all,

Wise to salvation was good Mistress Hall,

Something of Shakespeare was in that,
  but this

Wholly of him with whom she's now in
  bliss.[2]

Judith had three children, all of whom died before the age of 25 without having children. Susanna's daughter, Elizabeth, was Shakespeare's last living direct descendant. Elizabeth also had no children. With her death in 1670, the last of Shakespeare's line died.

Hamnet, and his parents, John and Mary. A monument close to his grave is inscribed with these words:

> *Good friend for Jesus sake forbear,*
> *To dig the dust enclosed here,*
> *Blest be ye man that spares these stones,*
> *And cursed be he that moves my bones.*[3]

It is recorded that Shakespeare wrote this himself.

Though he was admired and respected throughout his lifetime, William Shakespeare's legacy would grow beyond anyone's dreams after his death. His plays and sonnets would be translated into every written language. His plays would continue to be performed in theaters and playhouses. He would be regarded by many as the greatest dramatist ever to have lived. ⌐

Holy Trinity Church

Holy Trinity Church, where Shakespeare and all of his family are buried, is still an active church. Every year, the church holds a Shakespeare celebration in which people form a procession that winds its way through Stratford to lay flowers on the poet's grave.

This statue of William Shakespeare stands in Weimar, Germany.

TIMELINE

1557	1564	1569
John Shakespeare and Mary Arden are married in Aston Cantlow.	William Shakespeare is baptized in Stratford-upon-Avon, England, on April 26.	The Queen's Men and the Earl of Worcester's Men perform in Stratford.

Late 1580s	1592	1593
Shakespeare writes his first set of plays, the *Henry VI* trilogy.	Robert Greene insults Shakespeare in a pamphlet, the first known evidence of Shakespeare's life as a playwright in London.	Shakespeare publishes *Venus and Adonis* under the patronage of the Earl of Southampton.

1582	1583	1585
William Shakespeare and Anne Hathaway are married on November 30.	Susanna Shakespeare is baptized on May 26.	Twins Hamnet and Judith Shakespeare are baptized on February 2.

1594	1596	1597
Plague hits London. Shakespeare joins the Lord Chamberlain's Men. *The Rape of Lucrece* is published.	Hamnet Shakespeare dies and is buried in Stratford on August 11.	Shakespeare purchases New Place in Stratford on May 4.

TIMELINE

1598	1599	1601 or 1602
Dismantling of the Theatre begins on December 28.	Construction of the Globe Theatre is completed. Shakespeare moves to Southwark.	Shakespeare writes *Hamlet*.

1609	1611	1613
Shakespeare's Sonnets is published.	Shakespeare retires to Stratford.	The Globe Theatre catches fire and burns to the ground on June 29.

1603	1603–1606 (?)	1608
Queen Elizabeth I dies. James I becomes the patron of the Lord Chamberlain's Men.	Shakespeare writes *King Lear*.	The King's Men begin playing at the Blackfriars.

1616	1616	1623
Shakespeare alters his will to leave all of his estate to Susanna on March 25.	Shakespeare dies on April 23. He is buried in Stratford.	The first collection of Shakespeare's plays, the *First Folio*, is printed by Shakespeare's colleagues from the Lord Chamberlain's Men.

ESSENTIAL FACTS

DATE OF BIRTH

April 1564

PLACE OF BIRTH

Stratford-upon-Avon, England

DATE OF DEATH

April 23, 1616

PARENTS

John Shakespeare and Mary Arden

EDUCATION

King's New School

MARRIAGE

Anne Hathaway (November 30, 1582)

CHILDREN

Susanna, Judith, Hamnet

CAREER HIGHLIGHTS

In the late 1580s, Shakespeare wrote the *Henry VI* trilogy. His extremely successful play *Julius Caesar* was presented for the first time in the newly constructed Globe Theatre in September 1599. Shakespeare wrote his masterpiece, *Hamlet*, in 1601 or 1602. In 1603, King James I became the patron of the Lord Chamberlain's Men, requesting performances at his court 14 times a year.

Societal Contribution

During his lifetime, Shakespeare wrote a multitude of plays and sonnets that remain popular today. His works include famous plays such as *Hamlet*, *Romeo and Juliet*, and *Julius Caesar*.

Residences

Stratford-upon-Avon, England; London, England

Conflicts

After their landlord, Giles Allen, increased the rent for the Theatre, Shakespeare and the Lord Chamberlain's Men purchased their own land and hauled pieces of the Theatre to the new site, creating the renowned Globe Theatre.

Quote

"To be, or not to be, that is the question:

Whether 'tis nobler in the mind to suffer

The slings and arrows of outrageous fortune,

Or to take arms against a sea of troubles,

And by opposing, end them."—*From Shakespeare's* Hamlet

ADDITIONAL RESOURCES

SELECT BIBLIOGRAPHY

Ackroyd, Peter. *Shakespeare: The Biography.* New York: Doubleday, 2005.

Greenblatt, Stephen. *Will in the World: How Shakespeare Became Shakespeare.* New York: Norton and Company, 2004.

McDonald, Russ. "The Elizabethan Stage." *British Heritage.* June/July 2002.

Schoenbaum, Samuel. *William Shakespeare: A Compact Documentary Life.* Oxford: Oxford University Press, 1987.

Updike, John. "Late Works." *New Yorker.* 7 Aug. 2006.

FURTHER READING

Chrisp, Peter. *Welcome to the Globe: The Story of Shakespeare's Theatre.* New York: DK Children, 2000.

Donnermuth-Costa, Carol. *William Shakespeare.* Minneapolis, MN: Lerner Publishing, 2001.

Mannis, Celeste. *Who Was William Shakespeare?* New York: Grosset & Dunlap, 2006.

Turk, Ruth. *The Play's the Thing: A Story About William Shakespeare.* Minneapolis, MN: Carolrhoda Books, 1998.

Web Links

To learn more about William Shakespeare, visit ABDO Publishing Company on the World Wide Web at **www.abdopublishing.com**. Web sites about William Shakespeare are featured on our Book Links page. These links are routinely monitored and updated to provide the most current information available.

Places To Visit

Globe Theatre
21 New Globe Walk, Bankside, London, UK
44-(0)-20-7902-1400
www.shakespeares-globe.org
The reconstructed Globe Theatre closely replicates how it looked in Shakespeare's day. Visitors can see one of his plays performed and tour the UK's largest exhibition on Shakespeare's life in London, which is housed in the basement of the theater.

Royal Shakespeare Theatre
Waterside, Stratford-upon-Avon, Warwickshire, UK
44-(0)-1789-40344
www.rsc.org.uk
The Royal Shakespeare Company performs at this theater in Stratford-upon-Avon. They perform Shakespeare's plays in traditional and modern forms.

Shakespeare's Birthplace and Visitor Centre
Henley Street, Stratford-upon-Avon, UK
44-(0)-1789-204016
www.shakespeare.org.uk
In Stratford, the Shakespeare Birthplace Trust has preserved the Henley Street house, Anne Hathaway's birthplace, and other properties and gardens related to the Shakespeare family. Visitors can tour the houses and see exhibits.

GLOSSARY

ale
> A kind of beer.

bailiff
> A town administrator who authorizes activity and keeps order.

ballad
> A type of song in which the verses tell a story, such as a poem set to music.

bond
> A binding security or firm assurance.

descendent
> A person whose descent can be traced to a certain individual or group.

dramatist
> A writer of dramas; a playwright.

excommunicate
> To ban someone from participating in a church.

ferment
> A chemical change in organic material, as carbohydrates break down to carbon dioxide and alcohol.

guild
> A type of medieval organization made up of merchants or craftspeople.

hop
> A plant used in brewing beer.

monologue
> A long speech without interruption by an actor in a play.

parish
> A district with its own church, or the area surrounding a church in which people live and work.

recession
> A decline in the economy.

replica
> A recreation of something; a copy or a model.

revenue
> Income; money earned.

vicar
> The main priest or minister of a church.

vintner
> A wine merchant.

will
> A document that specifies what should be done with a person's possessions upon his or her death.

wool brogger
> An unauthorized, illegal dealer of wool.

Source Notes

Chapter 1. Who Was William Shakespeare?
None

Chapter 2. First Act
1. William Shakespeare. *"Merry Wives of Windsor*, Act I, Scene IV."
William Shakespeare: The Complete Works. New York: Gramercy Books,
1975. n.pag.
2. William Shakespeare. *"Romeo and Juliet*, Act II, Scene IV." *William
Shakespeare: The Complete Works*. New York: Gramercy Books, 1975.
n.pag.

Chapter 3. Growing Up in Stratford
1. William Shakespeare. *As You Like It*, ed. William Allan Neilson.
Chicago: Scott, Foresman and Company, 1903. n.pag.
2. Stephen Greenblatt. *Will in the World*. New York: Norton, 2004.
55.

Chapter 4. Troubles and Joys
1. William Shakespeare. *"A Midsummer Night's Dream*, Act II, Scene III."
William Shakespeare: The Complete Works. New York: Gramercy Books,
1975. n.pag.

Chapter 5. The Start of a New Life
1. William Shakespeare. "Sonnet 145." *William Shakespeare: The Complete
Works*. New York: Gramercy Books, 1975. n.pag.

Chapter 6. Leaving His Mark on London
1. Stephen Greenblatt. *Will in the World*. New York: Norton, 2004.
213.

2. A.H. Bullen. *The Works of Christopher Marlowe*. London: John C. Nimmo, 1885. Vol. 1. "Marlowe the Playwright." The Online Library of Liberty. 2 Oct 2007 <http://oll.libertyfund.org/index.php?option=com/content&task=view&id=618&ltmid=292>.

Chapter 7. Hamnet and *Caesar*
None

Chapter 8. The New Globe Theater
1. Samuel Schoenbaum. *William Shakespeare: A Compact Documentary Life*. Oxford: Oxford University Press, 1987. 208.
2. William Shakespeare. "*Julius Caesar*, Act 1, Scene 1." *William Shakespeare: The Complete Works*. New York: Gramercy Books, 1975. n.pag.
3. Samuel Schoenbaum. *William Shakespeare: A Compact Documentary Life*. Oxford: Oxford University Press, 1987. 208.

Chapter 9. Making His Mark
1. Jeremy Hylton. *The Complete Works of William Shakespeare*. Hamlet. The Tech. MIT. 15 Aug. 2007 < http://shakespeare.mit.edu/hamlet/hamlet.3.1.html>.

Chapter 10. A Final Bow
1. Stephen Greenblatt. *Will in the World*. New York: Norton, 2004. 145.
2. Michael Best. "Married Life." *Shakespeare's Life and Times*. Internet Shakespeare Editions. University of Victoria: Victoria, BC, 2001–2005. 2 Oct. 2007 <http://ise.uvic.ca/Library/SLT/life/children.html>.
3. Michael Best. "Shakespeare's Death." *Shakespeare's Life and Times*. Internet Shakespeare Editions. University of Victoria: Victoria, BC, 2001–2005. 2 Oct. 2007 <http://ise.uvic.ca/Library/SLT/life/death.html>.

Index

Index Continued

ABOUT THE AUTHOR

Emma Carlson Berne has written and edited more than a dozen books for young people, including biographies of such diverse figures as Christopher Columbus, Laura Ingalls Wilder, the Hilton sisters, and Snoop Dogg. She holds a master's degree in composition and rhetoric from Miami University. Emma lives in Cincinnati, Ohio, with her husband, Aaron.

PHOTO CREDITS

North Wind Photo Archives, cover, 3, 6, 21, 29, 44, 50, 53, 59, 60, 65, 69, 70, 78, 83, 96 (bottom), 98 (top), 99 (top); Edward Gooch/Getty Images, 11; By Permission of the Folger Shakespeare Library, 12, 25, 30, 40, 87; Getty Images, 22, 39, 49, 95, 96 (top), 97, 99 (bottom); Hulton Archive/Getty Images, 54, 88, 98 (bottom); David Thomson/AP Images, 73; Time Life Pictures/ Mansell/Getty Images, 77; Simon Ho, 91